In the CAR

Activity Book

Steve Martin

Illustrated by Putri Febriana

THIS BOOK BELONGS TO:

WIDE EYED EDITIONS

· CONTENTS ·

Driver's License

Imagine going on an exciting car journey—
and you're the driver!

There are two important things you need.

First, you need to fill out
your driver's license.

DRIVER'S LICENSE

First name: ....

Second name: ....

Date of birth: ....

Address: ....

....

Nationality: ....

Draw a picture of yourself
here. There are rules for
a driver's license photo—
no hats, no sunglasses,
and no smiling!

You also need a certificate to say that your vehicle is safe to drive. Fill in the certificate below and sign it.

CERTIFICATE

Date: ....

Type of car:

....

Color: ....

License plate: ....

What type of fuel does it use?

....

Is it safe to drive? Circle yes or no.   Yes/No

Signed by: ....

BUILDING A RACE TRACK

Use the space on the opposite page to draw a race track. It could be as tall as a skyscraper, it could have stunt jumps, or it could go underwater. It's up to you!

Here are some pieces of road you could include in your race track.

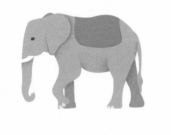

Here are some other things you could add around it, or you can make up your own.

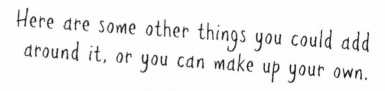

STOP!

GO!

Who's the Driver?

People need different types of vehicles. Draw a line to match the driver to their vehicle. One has been done for you.

Once you've matched the drivers to their vehicles, write a reason for each person's journey in the speech bubbles.

Stop that Car!

One of the vehicles in the picture on the right is breaking the speed limit! Use the clues below to find it. Cross out the vehicles as you eliminate them from your search, then circle the speeding vehicle when you find it.

SPEEDING TICKET

1. The vehicle is a car.
2. It isn't white.
3. It is all one color.
4. It isn't towing a trailer.
5. It is heading toward the highway.
6. It doesn't have a roof rack.

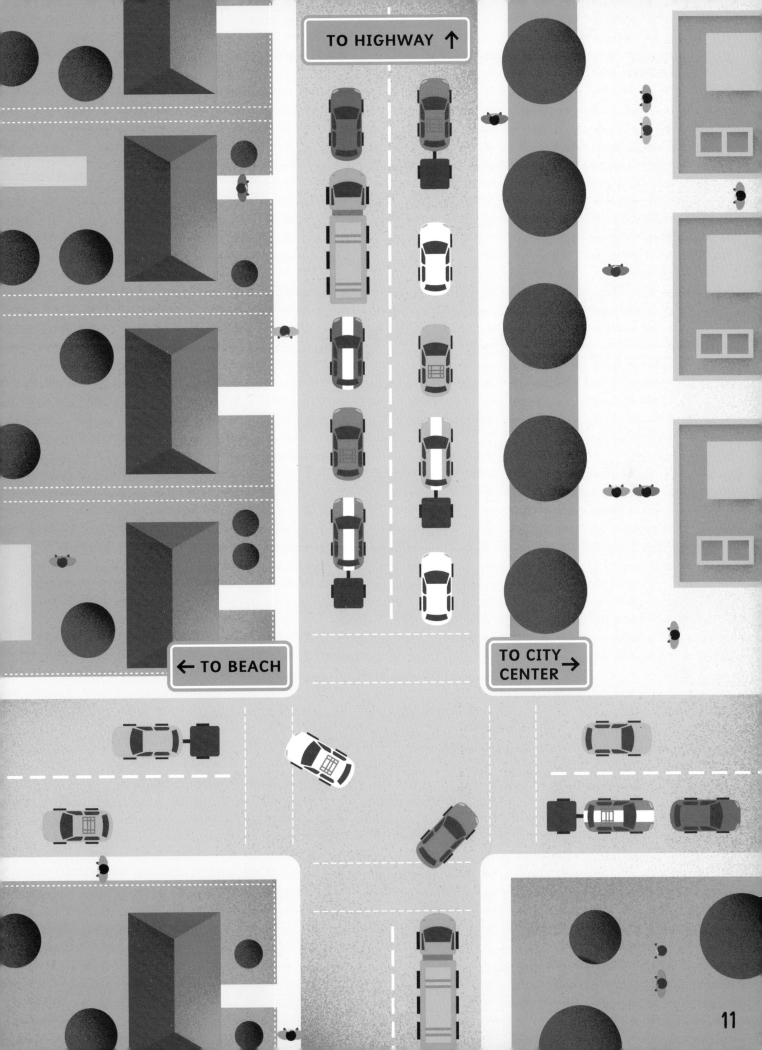

TO HIGHWAY ↑

← TO BEACH

TO CITY CENTER →

11

WHAT'S THE HOLDUP?

Oh no! There are problems on the road.
Look at each picture and write two short
stories about what has happened.

_____

_____

_____

_____

_____

_____

_____

_____

_____

_____

_____

_____

_____

_____

_____

_____

_____

_____

_____

Spot the Difference

Can you find ten differences between these two garages? Draw a circle around each one you find.

Rally Race

Can you find the rally car numbers in the grid below?
The numbers can go across, up, down, or diagonally.

Circle or highlight each number as you find it.

6	6	1	6	4	1	1	2
9	9	7	3	6	5	8	7
3	5	8	4	4	2	2	2
2	6	3	5	1	9	2	9
9	0	1	0	7	5	8	0
1	2	4	5	2	2	9	4
8	0	8	4	7	5	3	6
8	3	6	9	6	5	5	5

 107
 112
 290
 361
 422

 555
 661
 727
 808
 923

The Truck Stop

The trucks in this park are either yellow, red, green, or blue.

Complete this puzzle by drawing the trucks or writing their colors in the squares. Each color can appear only once in every row, column, and mini-grid.

color it in

This scene needs your skills to make it come alive with bright colors. Use pencils, crayons, or marker pens.

car Trip comic

Mariam has just been on a very exciting car journey.
In each box, draw what happened along the way.

We left our house during a fierce storm.

Soon, we were in the countryside. We drove past a beautiful forest.

Next, we passed through a big city. I saw enormous skyscrapers.

After driving for a long time, we stopped at a theme park. It had lots of exciting rides!

Finally, we arrived at our destination—a sandy beach, and a bright, blue sea.

What's wrong?

These people are driving to the beach.
But there are some things wrong with the
scene. Find and circle all eight things.

Welcome to
the Arctic

Color-by-Numbers

Color in all the numbered shapes using the key.

How many cars can you find? Write the number here. _____

Pack for the Trip

You are going to go on a long car journey. Below is a list of items to take with you—draw them in this bag.

* A snack
* A drink
* A game
* A book
* Crayons

Be a Detective!

Six friends are parked in a parking lot. Can you work out which car belongs to which driver? Solve the clues in order. Once you know the answer to each clue, write the driver's name beneath their car. One has been done for you.

1   2   3   4   5   6

Emma

Clues

1. Gene has a white car. It is not next to another white car.

2. Ava's car is parked between two white cars.

3. Ahmed's car is next to Gene's and no one else's.

4. Adam's car is red.

Gene

Maria

Ava

Adam

Ahmed

Emma

Did I Remember to Pack...?

It can be hard to remember everything you need when packing for a vacation. Look in the trunk of this car and circle objects on the list below to check you've packed them.

Checklist:

A cap
A camera
A pair of gloves
A soccer ball

A pair of sunglasses
An umbrella
A pack of crayons
A teddy bear

Sketch a Sports Car

Copy the picture of this sports car below onto the
grid on the right. Part of it has been started for you.
Draw it square by square, using the numbers as a guide.
Once you have finished, color in each car.

	1	2	3	4	5	6	7	8
A								
B								
C								
D								

What's Next?

Study these four sets of patterns. Can you work out which item is next in each list, and draw it in the space provided?

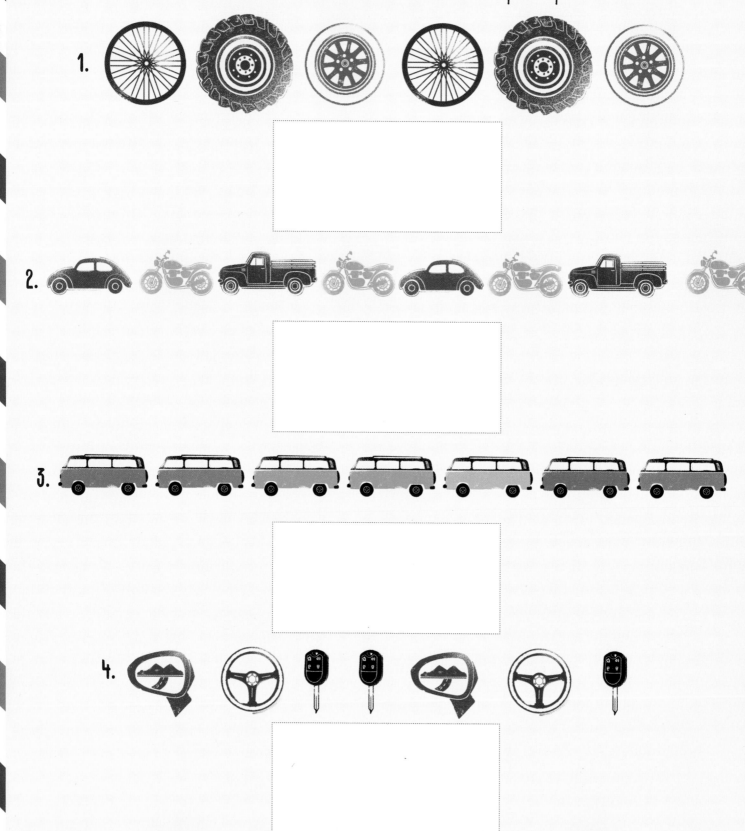

1.

2.

3.

4.

shortcut

This coach is taking people for a fun day out at the water park. Which road does it need to take to get there? Write your answer below.

The road that goes to the water park is ......

Add It Up!

These cars must catch the ferry but each car should only carry 12 lb of weight in total. Can you add up the weight on each car's roof rack, and cross out one item from each to give a total of 12 lb?

SERVICE STATION SEARCH

This service station is busy! Can you find and circle the eight things hidden in this scene?

- A piece of cheese
- A cup
- A flower
- A pair of green shoes
- A pencil
- An electric car
- A watch
- A bell

33

WATCH THE ROAD!

Drivers need to be aware of everything happening around them. Study this picture for one minute. Then cover it and answer the questions on the opposite page from memory. No peeking!

How much do you remember from the picture? Circle the correct answer.

1. Are you driving over 20 mph? .... YES / NO

2. Is your fuel tank empty? .... YES / NO

3. Are the traffic lights red? .... YES / NO

4. Is a man in a green shirt walking a dog? .... YES / NO

5. Is the moped red? .... YES / NO

6. Is there a hot-air balloon? .... YES / NO

* If you score 6, you are a very alert driver.
* If you score 4–5, you have good road awareness.
* If you score 3 or less, have another try!

CRAZY CARS

You're going to design your own car. Plan how it will look below, and then, on the right-hand page, put it all together.

WHEELS

Will the wheels of your car be circular, triangular, square, or another shape? Draw some options here.

BODY

What color will your car be? Do you want to give it a pattern?

EXTRAS

What extras will you give your car? It could have wings, a disco ball, or even a fish tank!

Use this space to put your planning
together and design your own car.

Around Town

Using the directions below, can you steer each car to where it needs to be? Use a pen or a pencil to draw the correct path. Once you've reached each destination, write the answer in the space provided.

BLUE CAR

- Drive straight, then take the first left turn after the swimming pool.
- Take the second right turn.

  The building on your right is

  _____

YELLOW CAR

- Take the first left turn.
- Take the first right turn and keep going until you cross the river.
- Take the first right turn.
- Take the first left turn.

  You arrive at

  _____

RED CAR

- Take the first left turn.
- Take the first right turn.
- Take the first right turn.

  The building on your left is

  _____

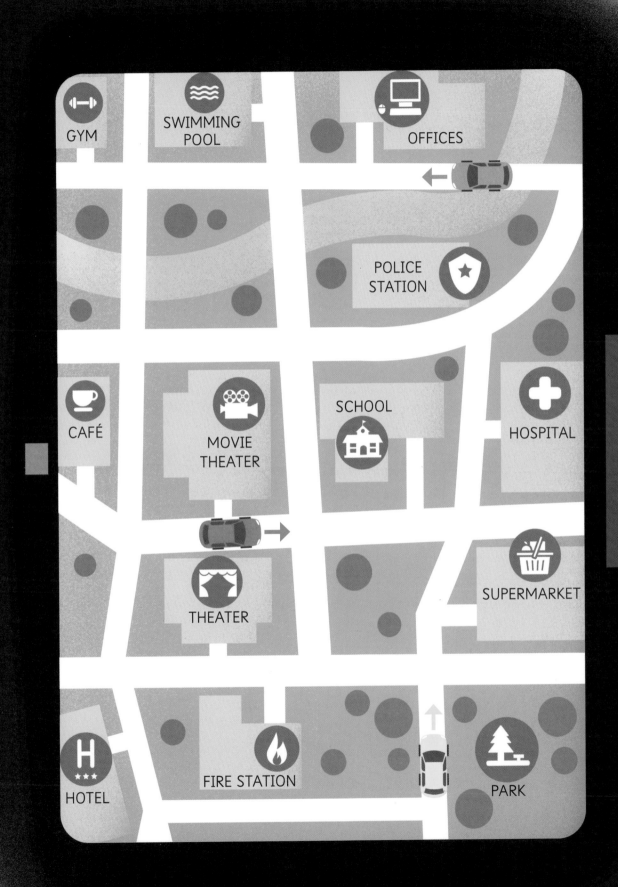

GYM

SWIMMING POOL

OFFICES

POLICE STATION

CAFÉ

MOVIE THEATER

SCHOOL

HOSPITAL

THEATER

SUPERMARKET

HOTEL

FIRE STATION

PARK

Dot-to-Dot

Connect the dots below to reveal why the spectators are so excited.

Taxi Turmoil!

These four people are waiting for their taxis to arrive.
Can you help them by matching the taxi to the passenger?

1

2

3

4

A ....

B ......1..........

C ....

D ....

My Crazy Journey

This game can be played alone, or with other people. Follow the prompts and fill in the blanks to create a story. Once you've filled in the blanks, read your story aloud. The sillier the words you choose, the funnier the story will be!

I drove my friend, _____, to the vet
(A famous person)

because their pet _____ had a bad cough.
(A type of zoo animal)

We all squeezed into the car and set off. I took a wrong turn and

ended up in _____ .
(A city)

I found the right road again, but there was another problem.

We drove straight into a hole in the road that was filled with

_____ and got stuck! I had to call
(Your favorite food)

_____ to come and help pull the car out.
(Someone you know)

Once we were free, we continued the journey. Suddenly, the weather

turned very bad, and it started raining _____ .
(A type of clothing)

Things got worse—my car got swept up by a tornado!

We swirled round and round, and landed on a beach. We were attacked

by a swarm of _____ .
(A type of insect)

We escaped by driving toward the sea but were swallowed by a

_____ . The creature burped and coughed
(A type of sea creature)

us up onto dry land.

managed to get back onto the road. There was a slight problem—an

enormous _____ was blocking our way.
(A type of vegetable)

The only way past was to eat our way through it!

After driving for _____ days, eventually, we arrived
(A number)

at the vets. While my friend's pet was being treated, I stayed outside in

the car. Parked next to me was a _____ with
(A type of vehicle)

a talking _____ behind the wheel. My friend
(A type of candy)

hopped back into my car. "Thanks for driving. Now that's done, let's go to

_____ ," they said.
(A fun place)

And off we went!

43

LUXURY LIMO

Design your dream limousine below. Draw some things inside, like a disco ball, your favorite snacks, or your friends. Then, choose some colors and fill in the scene.

Car Bingo

How many of these things can you see when you're out and about? Check the boxes as you see each one. It might take more than one car trip!

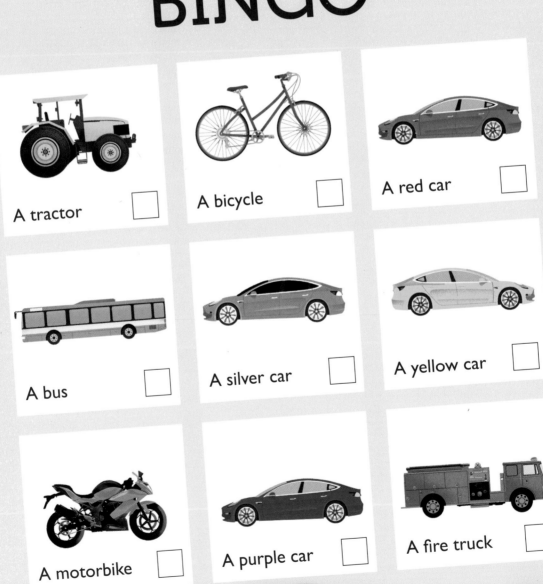

BINGO

A tractor ☐	A bicycle ☐	A red car ☐
A bus ☐	A silver car ☐	A yellow car ☐
A motorbike ☐	A purple car ☐	A fire truck ☐

BINGO

A taxi ☐

A sports car ☐

A truck with pictures ☐

A black car ☐

A digger ☐

A blue car ☐

A truck ☐

A cement mixer ☐

A green car ☐

47

AND THEN I...

Daniel is going to drive his new car. But he's forgotten the order he needs to do things in! Can you put these eight steps in the correct order?

Vehicle owner manual

Write "1" next to the first step, "2" next to the second step, and so on. The first one has been done for you.

Turn the engine off. - - - - -

Turn the engine on. - - - - - -

Park the car. - - - - - -

Get out of the car. - - - - - -

Drive down the road. - - - - - -

Fasten the seat belt. - - - - -

Get into the car. _1_ - - - - -

Unfasten the seat belt. - - - - - -

That Can't Be True!

Here are some interesting facts. But are they all real? Tick either the True or False boxes.

1. When Henry Ford made the Model T Ford car in 1908, he said that customers could have any color car they wanted, "so long as it is black."

True ☐   False ☐

True ☐   False ☐

2. It takes one minute for road-side mechanics to change all four tires of a Formula 1 race car during a race.

3. If you could drive there, it would take a full week of driving non-stop to reach the moon.

True ☐   False ☐

What's Hiding?

A picture of a vehicle is hidden in this grid.
Color the squares as listed below to find it.
One square has been done for you.

Brown: D8, D9

Red: C6, C7, C8, B8, B9

Blue: D6, D7, B6, B7

Yellow: F4, G4, H4, I4, J4, K4, L4, M4, N4, F5, G5, H5, I5, J5, K5, L5, M5, N5, F6, G6, H6, I6, J6, K6, L6, M6, N6

Black: E9, F9

Green: F7, G7, H7, I7, J7, K7, L7, M7, N7, F8, G8, H8, I8, J8, K8, L8, M8, N8, G9, H9, I9, J9, K9, L9, N9

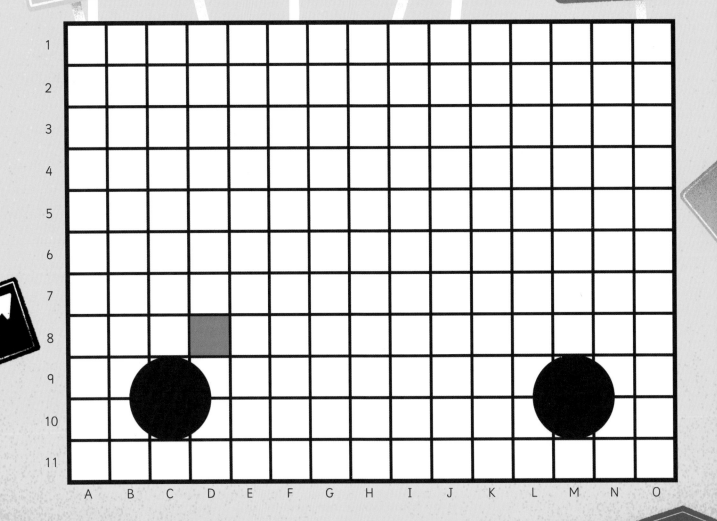

ODD ONE OUT

Look at all this traffic! Can you circle
the odd one out on each road?

1.

2.

3.

4.

Where Did I Put It?

Tim is working at the car wash, but he has lost all of his sponges! There are 14 sponges hidden in this picture. Can you find and circle them all?

Monster Trucks!

Monster trucks are cars with enormous wheels that can perform jumps and tricks. They are driven at performances called rallies. On the opposite page, design a poster to advertise a monster truck rally.

WHICH TRANSPORTER?

Which of these car transporters is identical to the example? Write your answer in the box below.

Example

The answer is:

Turn Left or Right?

You're driving home in the car, but there are roadworks everywhere! Can you get out of this maze and find a route back to your house?

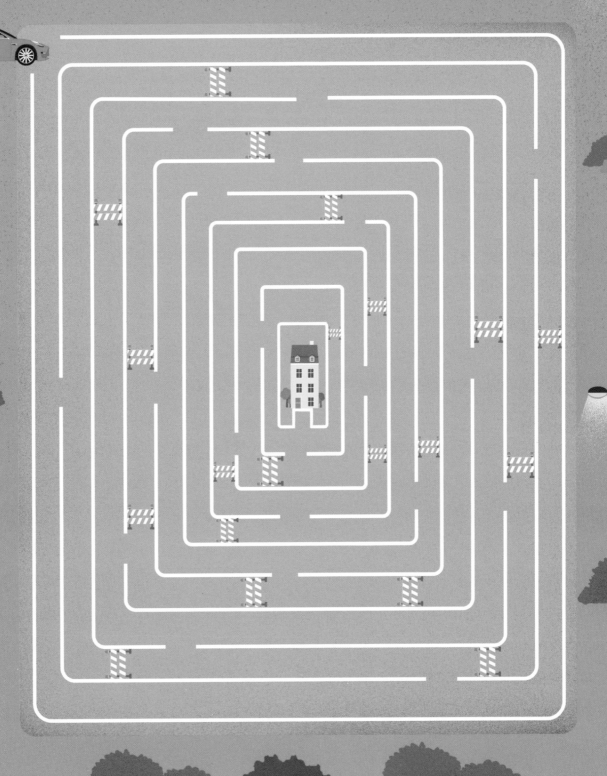

My Day of Travel

Fill in this keepsake diary of your trip. It can be real or imaginary!

Date: _ _ _ _ _ _ _ _ _ _ _ _ _ _

I got into my car, which was parked at _ .

I was traveling to _ .

I was traveling with _ .

The journey was _ _ _ _ _ _ _ _ _ _ _ hours long.

On the way, we drove past _

and _ .

We stopped off at _ for a snack.

The weather was _ .

When we arrived, I parked the car at _ _ _ _ _ _ _ _ _ _ _ _ _ _ _ _ _

_ _ _ _ _ _ _ _ _ _ _ _ _ _ _ _ and we got out.

The first thing I did after getting out of the car was:

_ _

_ _

My next trip will be by:

Bicycle/bus/boat/hot-air balloon

↖ Circle your choice.

Signed,

_ _

ANSWERS

PAGE 8: WHO'S THE DRIVER?

PAGE 10: STOP THAT CAR!

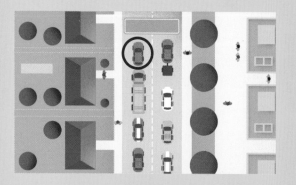

PAGE 14: SPOT THE DIFFERENCE

PAGE 16: RALLY RACE

6	6	1	6	4	1	1	2
9	9	7	3	6	5	8	7
3	5	8	4	4	2	2	2
2	6	3	5	1	9	2	9
9	0	1	0	7	5	8	0
1	2	4	5	2	2	9	4
8	0	8	4	7	5	3	6
8	3	6	9	6	5	5	5

PAGE 17: THE TRUCK STOP

60

PAGE 22: WHAT'S WRONG?

PAGE 23: COLOR-BY-NUMBERS

There are two cars in the picture.

PAGE 25: BE A DETECTIVE!

1. Ahmed
2. Gene
3. Ava
4. Maria
5. Emma
6. Adam

PAGE 26: DID I REMEMBER TO PACK...?

PAGE 30: WHAT'S NEXT?

1. Bike wheel

2. Green car

3. Pink van

4. Key

PAGE 31: SHORTCUT

The correct road to the water park is B.

PAGE 32: ADD IT UP!

1. 10 lb
2. 7 lb
3. 5 lb
4. 1 lb

PAGE 33: SERVICE STATION SEARCH

PAGE 34: WATCH THE ROAD!

1. No
2. No
3. Yes
4. Yes
5. No
6. Yes

PAGE 38: AROUND TOWN

Blue car: café
Yellow car: offices
Red car: hospital

PAGE 40: DOT-TO-DOT

PAGE 41: TAXI TURMOIL!

A: 3
B: 1
C: 4
D: 2

PAGE 48: AND THEN I...

1. Get into the car.
2. Fasten the seat belt.
3. Turn the engine on.
4. Drive down the road.
5. Park the car.
6. Turn the engine off.
7. Unfasten the seat belt.
8. Get out of the car.

PAGE 49: THAT CAN'T BE TRUE!

1. True
2. False. It takes around 4 seconds.
3. False. It would take 6 months.

PAGE 50: WHAT'S HIDING?

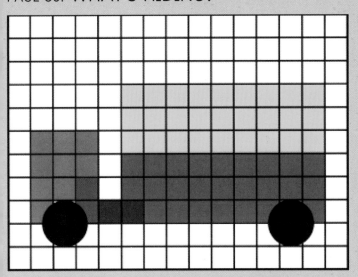

PAGE 51: ODD ONE OUT

1. Tractor (the others are construction vehicles)
2. Double-decker bus (the others have only one deck)
3. Taxi (the others are emergency vehicles)
4. Bicycle (the others have engines)

PAGE 52: WHERE DID I PUT IT?

PAGE 56: WHICH TRANSPORTER?

The matching transporter is A.

PAGE 57: TURN LEFT OR RIGHT?

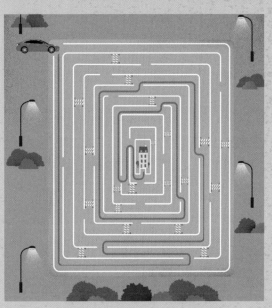

First published in 2021 by Wide Eyed Editions, an imprint of The Quarto Group.
The Old Brewery, 6 Blundell Street, London N7 9BH, United Kingdom.
T (0)20 7700 6700 F (0)20 7700 8066 www.QuartoKnows.com

A CIP record for this book is available
from the Library of Congress.

ISBN 978-0-7112-5648-4

The illustrations were created digitally

Published by Georgia Amson-Bradshaw
Designed by Kate Haynes and Elise Gaignet
Edited by Lucy Menzies
Production by Dawn Cameron

Manufactured in Guangdong, China TT012021

10 9 8 7 6 5 4 3 2 1